Easy Cook Book for Dads Who Don't Have a Clue!

Shirley Wheeldon

Recipes by Tim Johns

Illustrations

by

Mickey Wright

DB

DIADEM BOOKS

All Rights Reserved. Copyright © 2008 Shirley Wheeldon

No part of this book may be reproduced or transmitted in any form or by any means, graphic, electronic, or mechanical, including photocopying, recording, taping or by any information storage or retrieval system, without the permission in writing from the publisher.

Published by Diadem Books

For information, please contact:

Diadem Books
Ocean Surf
CLASHNESSIE
IV27 4JF
Scotland UK

www.diadembooks.com

Illustrations & cover by Mickey Wright
in association with Magical Memories.co.uk

ISBN: 978-0-9559741-8-2

Easy Cook Book for Dads Who Don't Have a Clue!

Also by Shirley Wheeldon

Pocket Size Handbook For Dads

Who Don't Have a Clue!

iUniverse 2008

ISBN 0-595-50999-1

The recipes in this book have been designed by our chef Tim, and tested by dads who now do have a clue.

For more information see

www.dadswhodonthaveaclue.com

Table of Contents

- Getting started — 1
- A guide to what we should eat — 4
- Start your day right — 8
- Light bites — 12
- Main course meals—what they should consist of — 20
- Meat meals — 21
- Fish meals — 40
- Vegetarian meals — 49
- Family meals — 59
- Desserts — 73
- A special meal for two! — 85
- Kids' lunch boxes — 91
- Tips — 95

Getting Started

So you thought you would never have to cook for yourself, let alone other people! Up to now you may have got away with everyone looking after you—Mum, girlfriend, wife, friends, business lunches and the staff restaurant at work; and you have every take away leaflet filed safely away ready for when you need it.

Then suddenly things change! For whatever reason, you have been asked to take some responsibility for keeping the family from starving or living on crisps and junk food. So it has fallen to you to provide Healthy nutritious food, but keeping within the shopping budget. Well, they don't ask much, do they?

Easy Cook Book for Dads Who Don't Have a Clue!

First things first. Have you any idea what a nutritious meal is? What should we eat to have a balanced diet?

Okay, so you may have heard talk of five portions of fruit and veg! Well, that's easy enough these days—all the shops advertise it. But what do you do with the fruit and veg when you have bought it? And yes, the shopping is up to you as well!

Making shopping lists

Sounds a bit boring, doesn't it? But it's better than making several trips to the shops because you forgot something or you have bought loads of things you really don't need. So look at the recipes and make the list—it really is worth it. Don't forget to check on the rest of the household needs, from washing up liquid to Clingfilm. Don't assume it's in the cupboards when you probably used it up and forgot to replace it.

Supermarkets

So you now have to form a very close relationship with a supermarket. You will need to memorise the floor plan of the store, learn a completely new skill, and yes, it really is difficult to wheel a wobbly trolley—and to feed a family you will need a trolley! There is also a protocol involved when shopping, keeping to the aisle routes, avoiding the walking pension books who are really only shopping to have a chat, and the children who are demolishing the stands. Then you will need to identify the areas that you will use. Remember the brands that you like, practice the art of packing the bags, and these day we use recycled 'bags for life.' Then you need patience to queue, and have to learn how to use the self-scan to pay.

That was the easy bit!

A Guide to What We Should Eat

THIS is the bit where we get serious, and you find some information on what to buy and what to avoid when shopping for the family.

Our diet should be *balanced*. That means we eat a variety of food that gives us all the nutrients we need to have a healthy body and lead an active life.

There are some basic rules and things you should be aware of. Each day you should try and eat a variety of foods from the five main food groups:

- Fruit (including fruit juices) and a variety of vegetables.

- Milk and dairy foods such as Yogurts.

- Bread, cereal (including breakfast cereals) and Potatoes (starchy foods).

- Meat.

- Fish.

Most people eat three meals a day and snack in-between. You should try and remember that, and should try and eat more fruit, vegetables and starchy foods. Drink less alcohol and reduce the amount of salt and sugar in your diet.

Watch out for labels on food packaging when shopping. Look for labels that say that it is low in fat, low in salt or sugar free. Sometimes things can be low in one area but very high in others, so beware. We need some fat in our diets, but *unsaturated fats* (found in nuts, seeds, avocados and olive and sunflower oil) is much better for us than the fat in cheese and those in some cakes and biscuits.

Fruit and vegetables are packed with vitamins and minerals, low in calories and high in fibre. How good is that! It's the easy way to get the family's diet right. With the bonus that eating lots of fruit and vegetables helps to keep the heart and body healthy. They are also good alternatives to eating crisps and chocolate as snacks between meals, so they also keep you and your family slim and active. So remember when you go shopping—BUY <u>A VAREIEY OF FRUIT AND VEGETABLES.</u>

Reduce the amount of salt and add flavour to your cooking by using herbs and spices, such as garlic, instead.

Swop the high fat snacks (such as crisps, biscuits etc) for a selection of chopped vegetables (you can buy them ready prepared from the supermarket if you are in a hurry). If you want a real treat, chocolate with less milk and more cocoa is actually better for you. It follows that plain chocolate is better for you than milk.

Choose drinks that are low in sugar. Watch out when stocking up on the family cold drinks! Remember to choose drinks that are low in sugar. Watch out for E numbers—it can really make the kids wild! Don't forget alcohol is high in calories and bad for your health if you drink too much.

Meat and dairy products are good as part of a healthy diet; however, choose leaner cuts of meat. Turkey is leaner than beef and can be used as an alternative in spaghetti bolognaise or in other recipes. Dairy products can contain a lot of fat, so when you are out and about shopping, look at the labels: try and choose skimmed or semi-skimmed milk instead of full fat, and go for low fat versions of cheese and yoghurts. Children should have higher fat contents in their diet, as they need calcium to build healthy teeth and bones.

Oily fish, like sardines and mackerel, contain omega-3 fatty acids, which can help to prevent heart disease and is good 'brain food' for kids. Try and avoid smoked fish, which often contains lots of salt.

Okay, so you now know what you should be buying, what to look for, and what to avoid; all you need now is the shopping list. So look at the recipes, check the cupboards, see what you need, write the list before you go to the supermarket, and make sure you write the amount of each item you need to buy. While you are making the list, just look in the cupboards and see if there is anything else you might need, things like cooking oil, tin foil, Clingfilm, and washing up liquid. Such items are regularly needed so you might as well top them up now rather than make a separate trip to the supermarket later.

♣

*Something to remember: if you are looking after a nursing mother, watch what they eat—it can affect the baby. For example: grapes for mum can give the baby tummy ache, so check if you are not sure.

Start Your Day Right

BREAKFAST, they say, is the most important meal of the day. But it is the easiest meal to miss by just having tea or coffee on the run.

Take time for a healthy breakfast—it is very important! It provides you with energy and helps to resist snacking before lunch.

Cereal, toast and fruit juice takes minutes to prepare and eat. You will feel better and snack less if you eat breakfast.

Here are some suggestions to make breakfast easy and fulfilling:

- Cereals are packed full of fibre and vitamins, but they also contain hidden extras such as salt and sugar, so it's back to reading the labels.
- Add dried or fresh fruit to your breakfast cereal. This can count as one of your five portions of fruit and vegetables which you should eat every day to keep you healthy.
- A small glass of fruit juice (150 ml) is also classed as one of your five.
- Half a grapefruit is good if you are on a diet.
- A bowl of fresh fruit and yogurt is another healthy option.
- Croissants with preserves (jam)—very continental!

So really, breakfast is very easy so you have no excuse for the family not to have breakfast.

Cereal bars are always handy if you are in a rush, but no real substitute for a proper breakfast.

Easy Cook Book for Dads Who Don't Have a Clue!

Remember, if the shopping is left for you to do, you should check the cupboard and if necessary buy:

Cereals, Milk, Yogurts, Bread, Fruit, Eggs—all are breakfast basics.

♣

If you fancy a cooked breakfast try:

Boiled eggs

You will need a pan of boiling water. (If you put a drop of vinegar in the water it will stop the egg cracking.)

Place 1/2 eggs in the pan of boiling water (best to put them in one at a time, using a large spoon to place them in the pan).

Boil for 2 mins – soft boiled, or up to 4 mins for hard-boiled.

Serve in eggcups with either hot buttered toast or plain buttered bread.

Scrambled eggs

Essential item is a **non-stick pan.**

Into a pan place about one teaspoon of butter or margarine; let this melt gently on a low heat.

Whilst the fat is melting, take a small bowl and break 2/3 eggs into the bowl. Take a fork or whisk and beat them until mixed. Season with salt and pepper. Add about one large spoon of milk.

Place two pieces of toast in the toaster.

Turn the heat up under the saucepan, and then add into the pan of melted butter the egg mixture you have just beaten in the bowl. With a wooden spoon keep stirring whist the eggs form together into a soft mixture and all the liquid has been absorbed. Turn off the heat,.

Butter the toast place on a plate, add the scrambled eggs on top .and enjoy.

But don't forget to put the pan in water afterwards, to soak! Scrambled egg can be a nightmare to get off, so you will be glad you used a non-stick pan.

Then of course there is the full English—but that's another story!

Light Bites

THESE can be meals we take to work, or meals we eat when not really hungry, but these snacks should still be healthy and nutritious.

The sort of things you just grab and go, have to be quick so it's all too easy to go for chocolate bars or a coffee and a cake. There are much healthier options.

Yes, we are back to fruit and nuts, which are, of course, easy to carry and easy to eat.

- Prepared fruit bowls and yogurts.

- Ready prepared Salad bowls are available from most supermarkets and some deli; even the fast food outlets do them now,

- Cereal and snack bars are of course another option.

When you actually add up the amount you spend each week on the light bites, you really will be surprised, so how about looking at Tim's ideas for things you can make without a lot of effort that will save you money?

Light bites are also the sort of things you eat while you are watching the footy, or a film. Or the sort of things that keep you and the family going in the middle of the day.

Right now you have been put in charge of what you and the family eat, so take a good look at the household weekly budget, what you and the family like to eat, and you will surprise yourself with what you can do—so go ahead give it a try.

Some Light Bite Recipes:

HOMEMADE MUSHROOM SOUP

Shopping list

- 1 punnet of button mushrooms
- 1 medium sized onion
- 1 clove of garlic
- 1 vegetable stock cube
- 1 small pot of double cream

- 1 tablespoon (large) of flour
- 3 oz butter
- Salt to season

Easy to prepare;

- cut mushrooms in ½
- peel and slice onion
- peel and chop garlic
- dissolve sock cube into 1pt of boiling water

Now let's get cooking!

- Melt butter in medium saucepan over a medium heat, and then add mushrooms, onions and garlic and fry until all ingredients are soft.
- Stir in flour until it coats ingredients and cook for 2 minutes
- Add the stock 1/3 at a time stirring constantly; once all is added, simmer for 20 minutes on a low heat, stirring occasionally.
- After 20 minutes add double cream; then remove from heat.

Light Bites

- Using either a food processor or a hand blender, carefully blend soup until smooth; add salt to taste.

Now to serve;

- Place soup in bowls and accompany with fresh crusty bread.

♣

POSH CHEESE AND TOMATO ON TOAST
(for 2 people)

Shopping list

- 1 punnet of cherry tomatoes
- 1 small wedge of mature cheddar (or a good quality cheese of your choice)
- 1 small red onion
- 1 egg
- 1 ciabatta loaf
- Salt and cracked pepper.

To prepare:

- Cut the cherry tomatoes in half.
- Peel and finely slice ½ the onion
- Grate 200g of cheese
- Cut ciabatta in ½ across width, then both 1/2s cut lengthways so you have 4 thin pieces.

Now to get cooking!

- Lightly toast all 4 pieces of ciabatta
- Put the cheese in a bowl then add, tomatoes and onion, and add just the yolk of the egg. Add a pinch of salt.
- Spoon the mixture of cheese etc over your ciabatta pieces, then spread evenly and grill until golden. Finish with a twist of black pepper.

SUPER B.L.T. SANDWICH
(makes 2 sandwiches)

Shopping list

- 1 packet of good quality back bacon (6 slices)
- 1 packet of baby gem lettuce
- 2 medium sized tomatoes
- 1 small jar of mayonnaise
- 1 small bottle of tomato ketchup.
- 4 slices of thick sliced bread.

Now to get prepared:

- 1/4 and wash lettuce, then shake off excess water and pat dry
- Slice tomatoes into 4's length ways.

Now to get cooking!

- Warm up a frying pan or griddle pan, then on a med/high heat fry bacon until cooked as you like it.

- Toast the bread on both sides, then on two of them spread mayonnaise and tomato ketchup on the other two.

- Place 4 slices of tomato on each mayonnaise pieces of bread

- Add a couple of leaves of lettuce on each.

- Then top each one with three pieces of bacon, and then top with the ketchupped pieces. Cut into 1/4s and enjoy.

♣

GARLIC MUSHROOM AND MOZZARELLA BRUSCHETTA
(SERVES TWO)

Shopping list

- 1 pack of field/portabello mushrooms
- 1 small red onion
- 1 ball of buffalo mozzarella
- 1 clove of garlic
- 1 ciabatta loaf
- 1 small jar of pesto.
- Olive oil

Light Bites

Now to prepare:

- Cut 2 mushrooms in ½ and then slice each ½ into small pieces.
- Peel and finely dice ½ the onion
- Peel and chop garlic
- Cut ciabatta in ½ width ways and then both pieces length ways

Now get cooking!

- Heat 2 dessert spoons (large) of oil in a frying pan over a medium heat, then add garlic and fry for 1 minute
- Then add mushrooms and onion and cook for approx 3 to 4 minutes until mushrooms are soft.
- Drizzle your bread with olive oil; then toast until golden.
- Place bread on plates, 2 each, and top with mushroom mix.
- Open mozzarella and drain of juice; then pull off little chunks and place as much of the cheese as you like on top (grill to melt if you want); then drizzle a teaspoon of pesto over each piece and serve.

Main Course Meals—What They Should Consist Of

Meat Meals

INCLUDING meat in the menu will often decide what vegetables and sauces are the best accompaniments for the meal. With practice you will soon know what goes with what, but for now just follow the ideas on the next few pages and then try experimenting yourself.

Meat is a good source of protein. It also contains a proportion of fat which we also need in our diets. In some recipes you might be asked to trim off the excess fat as some cuts have too much, which can be bad for you.

Turkey and Chicken are lean meats with very little fat.

Pork, lamb and beef are all higher in fat.

The supermarkets and butchers these days will trim the fat for you before you buy. In most supermarkets the meat is ready portioned and covered in film so you can see exactly what you are getting and you can count out the of portions before you get them home.

Some supermarkets even do the seasoning and have cooking ideas on the packet.

If you really want to cheat you can buy a ready cooked chicken from the supermarket, but that's not nearly as good as cooking for yourself, getting that fantastic smell as the meat cooks—and your mouth waters as you look forward to eating the meal you have worked so hard to prepare. So go on, give it a try, look at the recipes on the following pages and decide which one you want to try first. I know you can do it—just give it a try!

♣

Tasty Chicken Skewers with vegetable stir-fry:

Shopping list (makes 4 skewers for two people)

- 1 x packet of 2 chicken breasts
- 1 x Lemon
- 1 x Red pepper

- 1 x Red chilli   (Remember, they can be very hot!)

- 1 x Punnet of small mushrooms

- 1 x Jar of tikka spice/seasoning

- 1 x Small pot of natural yoghurt

- 1 x small bottle of sesame oil

- 1 x Bag of ready prepared stir fry vegetables

- Salt to season, you can use low salt if you prefer.

- 1x packet of bamboo skewers (you should be able to find in BBQ section of most supermarkets.

Now comes the tricky bit, so let's get organized and start to prepare the meal!

- Cut the raw chicken into 1" cubes. You will need a sharp knife and a cutting board. Put the chicken into a bowl. **Remember to Wash the board well as food poisoning can occur if you don't.**

- Cut and slice the lemon.

- Cut and dice the pepper into 1" pieces.

- Cut the chilli into half and remove the seeds; then chop into really small pieces.

- In a large bowl mix the Yogurt, chilli and two dessert-spoons (that's a large spoon) full of tikka spice together in the bowl; then add the chicken cubes. <u>Leave in the fridge for one hour to marinate</u>.

Now let's get cooking!

1. Thread a piece of chicken, then mushroom followed by a piece of pepper onto the skewer; continue until the skewer is full.

2. Turn on the grill, grease the bars on the grill tray with a bit of sesame oil, then place the skewers onto the grill tray and cook for 8-10 mins, turning them every 2 mins. When cooked, turn the grill off, but leave the skewers under the grill to keep warm.

3. In a large wok / frying pan, heat 2 dessert spoons (large spoons) of sesame oil; add the stir fry vegetables to the pan, with 2 pinches of salt. Fry the vegetables for 3-4 mins whilst you continue to stir the vegetables.

To serve

Place a mound of vegetables on each plate; place two skewers on top of the vegetables.

Then enjoy!

Here are some more easy-to-follow recipes for meat meals:

CHICKEN FRICASSEE WITH MUSHROOMS
(Serves 2)

Shopping list

- 2 chicken breasts
- 1 carrot
- 1 leek
- 1 medium onion
- 1 celery stalk
- 1 clove of garlic
- 1/2 lemon
- 1 bay leaf
- 6 mushrooms
- 2oz butter
- 2 table spoon (large) flour

- 1x glass med white wine
- 1 tub dried parsley
- 1 chicken stock cube
- 4 dessert spoons (large) of double cream
- salt and pepper to season.

To prepare:
- Cut up chicken into 1" cubes
- Peel and slice carrot
- Chop ½ the leek and wash
- Peel and dice onion
- Dice up ½ the celery
- 1/2 mushrooms
- Peel and chop garlic
- Squeeze the juice of ½ a lemon into a container.

Now let's get cooking!
- In a saucepan boil 2 pints of water, add carrots, onion, leek, garlic, celery and bay leaf.
- Simmer the vegetables for 20minutes

- Whilst the vegetables are cooking, heat a large spoonful of butter in a large saucepan over a medium heat. Place the chicken in the pan and fry off for 5 minutes, until lightly brown, then add the mushrooms and cook for further 2 minutes.

- After the vegetables have cooked for 20 minutes, scoop them out and place in a bowl, then strain off 1pt of the vegetable water into a jug; add to the stock cube, and stir in.

- To the chicken stir in the flour stirring constantly until a paste is formed around it. Stir in wine and cook for 1 minute.

- Slowly add the stock (as much as is required) stirring all the time until the a nice thick sauce is formed (spoon coating consistency).

- Then add all your cooked vegetables to the pan, the lemon and parsley, stir and simmer on a low heat for 10 minutes

- Add the cream and salt and pepper to taste.

To serve:

- Serve with rice, French fries or mashed potatoes.

STEAK WITH GARLIC AND ONION CREAM SAUCE
(serves 2)

Shopping list

- 2x thin cut sirloin steaks (approx 6 oz each)
- 1 clove of garlic
- 1 medium onion
- 1 tub of dried thyme
- 1/2 a lemon
- 150mls double cream
- olive oil
- salt and pepper

Now to get prepared:

- peel and chop garlic
- peel and thinly slice onion
- juice the lemon

Get cooking!

- In a medium frying pan heat up 2 dessert (large) spoons of olive oil on a high heat.

- Then place the steaks in and fry for 2 minutes each side; then remove and keep warm.

- Turn down the heat to medium, add 1 dessert spoon of oil and fry the onion and garlic for 3 minutes; then add 1 teaspoon of thyme and cook for 1 minute.

- Add the lemon and cream and stir in; put the steaks back in and simmer for 5 minutes, turning them once.

- Add salt and pepper to taste.

To serve:

- Accompany with a fresh salad and French fries or new potatoes and fresh vegetables.

Easy Cook Book for Dads Who Don't Have a Clue!

APPLE AND BLUE CHEESE CHOPS

Shopping list:

- 2 x pork chops
- 1 small onion
- 1 red apple
- 2 oz stilton
- 1/2 glass apple juice
- 150 ml double cream
- 1 tub dried sage
- Olive oil
- Salt and pepper

Now to get prepared:

- Peel and slice onion finely
- Finely dice apple leaving skin on
- Grate cheese

Now to get cooking!

- In a large frying pan heat 1 dessert spoon of olive oil over a medium heat, add the chops and fry for approx 12-15 minutes, turning a couple of times.

- Add onion and cook for 2 minutes; then add the diced apple, a sprinkling of dry sage and the apple juice; then simmer for 2 minutes. Then add the cream and simmer for a further 4-5 minutes until cream has thickened (coating consistency).

- Add the grated cheese and stir in until melted.

- Salt and pepper to taste.

Now to serve

- Serve with mashed potatoes and vegetables or simply with chips.

BAKED LAMB CUTLETS WITH ROASTED VEGETABLES AND SWEET POTATO
(serves 2)

Shopping list

- 6x lamb chops
- 1 sweet potato
- 1 red pepper and 1 green pepper
- 1 small courgette
- 1 medium red onion
- 1 small aubergine
- 2 garlic cloves
- 1 tub dried rosemary
- Olive oil
- Salt and pepper

To prepare:

- Pre heat oven at gas mark 6 or 200 deg c
- Peel and dice potato into 1" pieces

- Dice peppers into 1" pieces (remove the seeds and throw away)

- Slice courgette into 1" slices

- Dice ¼ aubergine into 1" pieces

- Peel and dice onion into 1" pieces

- Peel and slice garlic

Now to get cooking!

- On an oven tray place all your diced vegetables and potatoes, 1 teaspoon (small) of rosemary and garlic and drizzle with olive oil; then with your hands, mix all the ingredients together. Then sprinkle with salt and pepper to season.

- Place the tray of vegetables into oven and roast for 15 minutes.

- In a large frying pan heat 1 dessert spoon of oil over a high heat and fry your chops for 1-2 minutes on each side until brown.

- Season chops with salt; then place on top of your vegetables in oven and roast for a further 8-10 minutes.

To serve:

- Serve simply with salad and crusty bread or rice.

PANFRIED TURKEY STEAKS WITH LEMON GLAZE AND MANGE TOUT
(Serves 2)

Shopping list

- 2 x lean turkey steaks
- 1 dessert spoon of runny honey
- 2 lemons
- 1 red onion
- 1 punnet of beansprouts
- 1 packet mangetout
- 1 bottle soy sauce
- 1 garlic clove
- 1 tub of dried ginger powder
- Olive oil

To prepare:

- Cut the turkey steaks into 4 pieces.
- Zest (use the fine part of a grater) and juice (squeeze) the lemon.
- Peel and slice onion.
- Peel and slice garlic.

Now to get cooking!

- Heat 1 dessert spoon of oil in a large frying pan or wok, add the turkey steaks and fry for 2 minutes.
- Into the frying pan add, onion, garlic and ½ a teaspoon of ginger powder, and then cook for a further minute.
- Add lemon zest, lemon juice and a dessert spoonful of honey, and then simmer until it becomes sticky. Add the mangetout and a handful of beansprouts into the pan and cook for 1 minute,
- Add a few dashes of soy sauce and serve.

Now to serve:

- Accompany with boiled rice or noodles (both can be found in ready cooked pouches to microwave).

SWEET AND SOUR CHICKEN (SERVES 2)

Shopping list

- 2 chicken breasts (use 1 packet quorn pieces for vegetarian version)
- 2 cloves of garlic
- 1 bottle tomato ketchup
- 1 can of pineapple chunks
- 1 red pepper and 1 green pepper
- 1 red onion
- 1 bottle of soy sauce
- 2 dessert spoons of runny honey
- 1 packet of cornflour
- 1 small bottle of sesame oil
- 1 bottle of vinegar

To prepare:

- Cut the chicken into 1" chunks.

Meat Meals

- Dice the peppers into 1" chunks (remove the seeds and throw away).

- Peel and dice onion into1" chunks.

- Peel and slice garlic.

- Open can of pineapple and drain off juice into a small bowl.

- Into a mixing bowl add 3 dessert spoons of vinegar, 2 dessert spoons of honey, 4 dessert spoons of ketchup, 2 dessert spoon of corn flour and stir until smooth.

- Put pineapple juice into a measuring jug and make up to 6fl oz with water, then add to mixing bowl and stir in.

- In a frying pan heat 1 dessert spoon of oil and fry chicken for 3-4 minutes until golden.

- Add onion and peppers to the pan and fry for 4 minutes.

- Then add the mixture in the bowl and the pineapple chunks and simmer until thickened, stirring all the time; simmer for further 3 minutes and serve.

Now to serve:

- Serve with rice or noodles (available in microwave pouches to save time).

HOMEMADE BURGER WITH BBQ RELISH

Shopping list

- 227g or 8 ounces lean beef mince
- 1/2 small red pepper
- 1 tomato
- 1 medium onion
- 1 tub of dried parsley
- Bottle of bbq sauce
- Teaspoon of English mustard
- 1 beef stock cube
- 2 crusty baps
- A bag of mixed salad leaves
- Salt and pepper
- 1 egg
- Olive oil

Now to get Prepared:

- Peel and finely dice the onion

- Finely dice the peppers (remove the seeds and throw away)

- Finely dice tomato

Now to get cooking!

- Into a mixing bowl put the mince add onion, pepper, egg, ½ teaspoon parsley, ground stock cube, and a teaspoon of English mustard and mix together.

- Add 2 pinches of salt and a pinch of pepper and mould into 2 burgers.

- In a pan heat one dessert spoon of olive oil over a medium heat, place in burgers and cook for 4-5 minutes each side.

- Whilst cooking, place in a small bowl the tomato and one dessert spoon of bbq sauce and mix together.

- Slice baps in half and toast on the bottom of the bap; place a couple leaves of lettuce on each half.

- When the burger is cooked place on top of lettuce, add a spoon of tomato relish to each burger and place the other half of the bap on.

Now to serve:

- Accompany with French fries or potato wedges.

Fish Meals

F**ISH** meals are highly nutritious and a healthy option which we should explore, and try new varieties of fish other than the basic well known varieties.

This can be a little tricky! Yes, the kids like fish fingers; you have tried a prawn cocktail or a prawn curry after the match, and even the odd bit of salmon with hollandaise sauce. That's probably all you know. In fact, it's all a lot of people know.

Fish Meals

The fish counter at the supermarket is not always the easiest place to shop. Let's face it, there is that funny smell, all those fishy eyes looking at you and the fishmonger can look a bit menacing with his big knife slicing away all the inners and everything. Kids, however, love to look at the lobsters and crabs.

Fish comes in many forms—fresh from the fishmonger or fish counter at the supermarket.

Pre-packed fresh fish with all the bits nicely trimmed off that you don't want,

Or frozen in bags, when you just take out the portion you want.

Then of course there are the ready meals. Not that they actually have a lot of fish in them.

And for the kids, both big and small, fish fingers.

Fish sticks are good for the kids' lunch boxes.

Oily fish is an excellent source of omega 3. Indeed, fish oils are very good for you.

Fish is low in fat and good if you are on a diet.

Why not try something different? Sea bream, trout, and mackerel—there are loads of different types to try.

So now you know all that, give the following recipes a try, and if you can get the kids to try fish, remember, it's really good for them.

Simple grilled Salmon, new potatoes, salad and pesto

Shopping list

- 1 x pack of Salmon steaks (without bones)
- Olive oil
- 2oz (50g) of butter
- Salt and pepper
- 1 x Lemon
- 1 x Jar of Pesto
- 1 x Bag of small new potatoes
- 1 x Bag of mixes salad leaves
- 2 Tomatoes
- Half a cucumber
- 1 x small red onion.

Fish Meals

Now to prepare

1. Wash the salad leaves in cold water, then place in a colander to drain for about 5 mins.

2. Then give the colander a shake to remove the excess of water

3. With a sharp knife, cut the tomatoes into six pieces.

4. Slice the cucumber thinly (as many slices as you like).

5. Peel and finely slice half of the red onion.

Now Let's get cooking!

1. Turn on the grill.

2. Put the potatoes into a saucepan (as many as you require) and cover with boiling water, from a pre-boiled kettle. Add salt and boil until cooked. To check if the potatoes are cooked, stab the largest potato with a small knife, and it should go in easily. This should take 10-15 mins according to size.

3. Place the salmon pieces onto the grill tray, season each portion with a pinch of salt and pepper; then squeeze half of the lemon over the salmon, and put a knob of butter on each one.

4. Place under the grill and cook for 10-12 mins. Turn of the grill and leave for 2 mins.

5. Drain off the potatoes.

To serve

Place the salad and the potatoes onto a large dining plate. Then, using a fish slice (that's the flat one), remove the salmon from the grill tray and put on the plate; squeeze the other half of the lemon over the salmon. Serve with a teaspoon (small spoon) of pesto.

♣

And now some more easy-to-prepare fish recipes:

GRILLED PLAICE WITH PRAWN AND GARLIC BUTTER
(SERVES 2)

Shopping list

- 2 x 2 6oz plaice fillets skinned
- 3oz cooked prawns
- 1 garlic cloves

- 3oz butter
- 1/2 lemon

To prepare:

- Peel and slice the garlic
- Juice the lemon

Now to get cooking!

- In a frying pan melt half the butter and place in the plaice fillets; cook for 2 minutes on each side.
- Add the garlic and the prawns and cook for a further minute.
- Squeeze in the lemon juice and add the rest of the butter.
- When the butter has melted, serve.

To serve:

- Serve with new potatoes and salad.
- Or simply with chips.

GRILLED SMOKED HADDOCK WITH SPINACH AND POACHED EGG
(Serves 2)

Shopping list

- 2 x 6oz smoked haddock fillets
- A bag of washed spinach
- 2 eggs
- 2oz butter
- Salt and pepper
- 1 tub of ground nutmeg

To prepare

- Pre heat the grill

Now to get cooking!

- On a greased grill tray place the smoked haddock and grill for 5 minutes; then turn off and leave under the grill to keep warm.

Fish Meals

- In a saucepan boil one pint of water, add 2 eggs and poach slowly for 3 minutes; remove and place onto kitchen paper.

- In a frying pan heat the butter, a pinch of nutmeg, then add the spinach and cook until all the spinach is wilted.

- Season spinach with salt and pepper to taste.

Now to serve

- Place spinach in the centre of the plate, top with a piece of the smoked haddock, and then add the egg.

- Accompany with fresh salad or new potatoes.

♣

SPICY PRAWN STIR FRY WITH PEANUTS (SERVES 2)

Shopping list

- 1 packet of cooked peeled king prawns (use quorn for vegetarian version)

- 1 x packet of unsalted peanuts

- 1 packet of ready prepared stir fry vegetables

- 1 bottle of soy sauce

- 1 Chili
- 1 garlic clove
- 1 tub of ground ginger
- 1 pouch of ready cooked noodles
- 1 bottle of sesame oil

Now to get prepared

- Peel and slice garlic.
- Half and deseed the chili and slice finely. (Throw the seeds away).

Now to cook!

- Heat 2 dessert spoons of sesame oil in a wok or large frying pan; add the garlic and prawns and fry for 1 minute.
- Add vegetables, ground ginger and the finely sliced chili and fry for a further 2 minutes, then add ½ packet of peanuts.
- Add noodles and stir in, then add 4 dessert spoons of soy sauce and 2 dessert spoons of water and warm through.

To serve:

- Place a mound of the mixture into the centre of each plate and drizzle with sesame oil.

Vegetarian Meals

VEGETARIAN meals, although seen to be different, will appeal to people of all tastes. In fact, most people will try the vegetarian option at a BBQ and enjoy it very much. People do not always understand how satisfying vegetarian food can be.

These days the supermarkets stock a good variety of ready prepared quorn products—mince, chicken-type pieces for stir-fries etc., nut roasts as well as sausages, burgers. These can be found in both the chilled cabinets and the freezer section.

Cheese is a good basic item for the fridge and a wide variety is available in any supermarket.

Readymade Quiches served with either salad or chips make a quick and easy meal. These are readily available in supermarkets. For something special, try the farm shops or local farmers markets.

Eggs—you will be amazed what you can do with eggs! Delicious omelettes with a variety of fillings, including Spanish omelettes, make a substantial meal.

Very Quick and Easy Tomato and Cheese Pasta (serves two)

Shopping list

- 1 x packet of dried Penne or Fussilli pasta.
- 1 x Jar of Napolitaine-style tomato sauce (in the pasta section at the supermarket).

Vegetarian Meals

- 1 x small onion.
- 1 x pot of dried thyme.
- 1 x small wedge of Parmesan cheese.
- 1 x courgette
- Olive oil

Easy to prepare:

- With a sharp knife peel and dice the onion.
- Dice the courgette into small pieces.
- Grate the parmesan cheese into a small bowl.

Now to the cooking—it's really easy!

- Into a large pan of slightly salted boiling water, place 6oz of pasta. Cook for 15mins until soft.
- Drain the pasta into a colander over the sink; then leave to stand over the saucepan.
- In a large frying pan, heat 1 dessert (large) spoon of olive oil over a medium heat. Then fry the onion and courgettes until soft.
- Add one teaspoon (small) of thyme and cook for 2mins.
- Add the pasta sauce to the frying pan with the onions and courgettes and simmer for 5 mins.
- Add the pasta to the sauce and stir in.

To serve

Place the pasta in two large bowls and sprinkle with parmesan cheese. You may like to serve with crusty or garlic bread.

♣

More Vegetarian Recipes:

QUICK AND EASY VEGETABLE LASAGNE

Shopping list

- 1 courgette
- 1 aubergine
- 1 red onion
- 4 mushrooms
- 1 yellow pepper
- 1 cup frozen peas
- 1 packet quick cook lasagna sheets
- 1 tin chopped tomatoes
- 1 clove garlic

- 1 tub tomato puree
- 1 tub of dried basil
- 1 jar of ready-made white sauce
- 2oz cheddar cheese
- Olive oil
- Salt and pepper

Now to get prepared:
- Slice the courgette
- Dice ½ the aubergine (1"pieces)
- Peel and dice the onion
- Slice mushrooms
- Dice peppers into 1" pieces. (Remove the seeds and throw away.)
- Peel and chop the garlic
- Grate the cheese
- Open the tin of tomatoes

Now get cooking!

- In a large frying pan heat 2 dessert spoons of oil, then add the garlic and all of the vegetable ingredients and fry for approx 5 minutes until soft and lightly coloured.

- Pour the tomatoes into the pan, and add 1 dessert spoon of tomato puree and 1 teaspoon of basil; pour in ¼ pt of water, then stir and simmer for 15 minutes; add salt and pepper to taste.

- Allow mix to cool for 20 minutes.

- Take an ovenproof dish approx 10"x8" and place a layer of vegetable mix, top it with a layer of dried pasta and repeat process.

- Then pour over the last layer of pasta, a jar of white sauce, smooth out and top with grated cheese.

- Bake in a preheated oven on gas mark 6 or 200 degrees c for 25 minutes.

Now to serve:

- Accompany with a mixed salad, garlic bread or potato wedges—or all, if you're that hungry!

Vegetarian Meals

CHEAT'S QUORN CURRY

Shopping list

- 1 packet of quorn pieces
- 1 medium onion
- 1 packet of fresh coriander
- 1 large carrot
- 1 courgette
- 1 red pepper
- 1 sweet potato
- 1 x400ml jar of a good curry sauce. (Korma is mild, bhuna is medium, jalfrezi is hot, vindaloo is very hot.)
- 1 small pot of natural yoghurt
- Salt and pepper
- Olive oil

To prepare:

- Peel and slice onion
- Dice courgette into 1" pieces

- Peel and slice carrot

- Dice pepper into 1" pieces (remove the seeds and throw away)

- Peel sweet potato and dice ½ into 1" pieces

- Chop 2 dessert spoons of coriander

Now get cooking!

- In a wok or large frying pan, heat 2 dessert spoons of oil and fry off all your vegetables for approx 5 minutes until start to colour; add a pinch of salt and pepper.

- Add the jar of sauce and stir in, then simmer for 15 minutes.

- Stir in 2 dessert spoons of yoghurt, and sprinkle with the coriander.

Now to serve:

- Serve with boiled rice and naan bread.

Vegetarian Meals

PANFRIED HALOUMI CHEESE WITH BAKED VEGETABLES AND PESTO

Shopping list

- 1 packet haloumi cheese
- 1 carrot
- 1 red onion
- 1 parsnip
- 1 red pepper
- 1 jar of pesto
- 2oz flour
- Olive oil
- Salt and pepper

Now to get prepared:

- Open haloumi cheese and slice into 4 pieces
- Peel and slice carrot
- Peel and dice onion

- Peel and dice parsnip

- Dice up pepper. (Remove the seeds and throw away.) Try and keep vegetables all the same size.

- Put flour on a small plate

- Preheat oven gas mark 6 or 200 c

Now to get cooking!

- Put all your vegetables into an oven tray, drizzle with oil and sprinkle with salt and pepper; mix all together.

- Place in oven and bake for 20 minutes.

- 5 minutes from the end of your vegetables being cooked, heat 2 dessert spoons of oil in a frying pan over a medium heat.

- Place each piece of cheese in the flour and coat, tapping off any excess flour.

- Fry the cheese for 2 minutes, turning a few times until golden.

Now to serve

- Place a mound of vegetables in the centre of a plate, top with 2 slices of cheese and drizzle with pesto (as much as you like); serve simply with salad.

Family Meals

SITTING round a table and enjoying a great meal is the key to being a family. It's time to talk about your day, the things that have gone wrong, things that have made you laugh. It instils good manners in children, which then makes going out for a meal a pleasant experience for everyone.

If you can establish a good eating pattern for your family it really will make a difference later in life. Try and avoid children browsing and snacking on crisps and sweets throughout the day. That way, when it comes to meal times, everyone is hungry and will enjoy the meals you have worked so hard to prepare for them.

Portion sizes can be an issue—remember, children don't eat as much as adults.

Do try not to make an issue if someone is on a special diet; just try and incorporate it into the meal plan for that day without any fuss.

It is much better to put items of food onto a child's plate that they like and enjoy, and then add a very small amount of a new item for him/her to try. Children follow by example and if you are sitting round a table together, they can see you eating different foods and will often ask to try.

If they don't like something the first time, it's well worth reintroducing it at a later date, disguising vegetables by grating carrots onto a salad. Adding finely chopped courgettes and peppers into a pasta sauce is another option you might like to try. If they can't really see it they will probably eat it.

Fussy eaters get worse if you make a fuss about it, so encourage them to eat by setting an example; try and sit together at a table and make meal times enjoyable for you all.

Tim's recipes set out to do just that.

Easy Spaghetti Bolognese
(Serves two)

Shopping list

- 200g Lean mince beef, turkey (or quorn if vegetarian)
- 1 x Medium onion
- 1 x Tube of tomato puree
- 1 x Pot of dried mixed herbs
- 1 x Jar or garlic puree/paste
- 1 x Packet of dried spaghetti
- 4 x Mushrooms
- 0live oil
- 1 x can of chopped tomatoes
- 1 x Beef stock cube (or vegetable)
- Salt and pepper to season
- 1 x Small wedge of parmesan cheese (optional)

Easy to prepare:

- Peel and slice the onion and mushrooms.
- Dissolve the stock cube into a jug, with ¾ pint of boiling water.
- Grate the parmesan cheese into a dish.

Let's get cooking!

- Heat 1 dessert spoon (the large one) of olive oil into a wok or large frying pan. Fry the mince until it is brown, stirring it with a wooden spoon to break up the mince into small pieces.
- Add the chopped onion and mushrooms and cook for a further 5 mins.
- Add the chopped tomatoes, the liquid stock and one dessert (large) spoon of tomatoes puree. Then simmer on a low heat for about 20 mins.
- After the mince has been cooking for 10 minutes, with the meat simmering, it is time to cook the spaghetti. In a large pan, filled with plenty of boiling, slightly salted water, add the spaghetti (follow the instruction on the packet for cooking times as each brand can be different).
- Once the spaghetti is soft, drain in a colander over the sink.
- Season the Bolognese sauce by seasoning as required with salt and pepper.

To serve

Place the desired amount of spaghetti in the centre of a large plate and top with a generous portion of Bolognese, and top sprinkle with parmesan cheese. You may also like to add some crusty or garlic bread.

One pot sausage casserole
(serves two)

Shopping list

- 1 x packet of thick sausages (you can substitute with Quorn if you are vegetarian)
- 2 x fresh Carrots
- 1 x small leek.
- 4 x mushrooms
- 1 x Red pepper
- 1 x large jacket size potato
- 1 x small can of kidney beans
- 1 x tube of tomato puree
- 1 x can of chopped tomatoes
- 1 x chicken or vegetable stock cube
- 1 x pot of dried sage
- Salt and pepper to season
- Olive oil
- 1 small crusty French stick

Easy to prepare!

- With a sharp knife, peel and slice the carrots.
- Wash and then slice the leeks.
- Cut the mushrooms into ¼ with a sharp knife.

- Dice the pepper into small pieces.
- Peel and dice the potatoes (small cubes about 1" in size)
- Open the can of kidney beans, then drain and wash in cold water to remove the slime.
- Dissolve the stock cube into ¾ pint of boiling water.

Let's get cooking the easy way!

- Heat 1 dessert spoon (large) of olive oil in a large frying pan, or wok. Then, on a low to medium heat, fry the sausages for 3-4 min's until brown.
- Add all of the vegetable ingredients into the pan and stir, and cover for 5 mins, stirring occasionally.
- Add the chopped tomatoes, 1 teaspoon (small) of sage, and the tomato puree and the liquid stock to the pan. Then simmer for a further 15 mins, stirring occasionally.
- Add the kidney beans, season with salt and pepper and continue to simmer for another 10 mins

To serve

Simply dish up a portion of the casserole to each person, with crusty bread.

Family Meals

TASTY COTTAGE PIE
(serves 4)

Shopping list:

- 1x400g pack of lean beef mince
- 1x large onion
- 2 carrots
- 2 celery sticks
- 6 button mushrooms
- 1 clove of garlic
- 1 beef stock cube
- 1 small bottle of Worcester sauce
- 1 tube tomato puree
- 2 oz flour
- Salt and pepper
- 4 large potatoes
- 2oz butter

To prepare:

- Peel and finely chop onion
- Peel and dice carrots (1cm dice)

- Wash and dice the celery (1cm)
- Slice mushrooms
- Peel and chop garlic
- Peel and cut potatoes into 1" dice
- Dissolve stock cube into 1pt of boiling water

Now to get cooking!

- Heat a large frying pan or wok over a medium heat, add the mince and fry for 5 minutes breaking mince up with a wooden spoon.
- Add garlic and vegetables to the mince and cook for 5 more minutes stirring occasionally.
- Now add 2oz of flour and 1 dessert spoon of tomato puree, then stir in until it forms a paste around mixture.
- Add the beef stock and a couple of dashes of Worcester sauce to the pan, and stir over a low heat for 3 minutes until mix starts to thicken.
- Simmer over a low heat for 15 minutes stirring occasionally; add salt and pepper to taste.
- Turn off place in an oven proof dish (approx 10"x8") and let cool for 30 minutes.

Family Meals

- In a large saucepan place the potatoes, and cover with boiling slightly salted water, then boil the potatoes for approx 15 minutes till they are soft.

- Drain off potatoes and mash until smooth.

- Add butter to the potatoes and stir in.

- Cover mince with potatoes and spread evenly with a fork; bake in a preheated oven gas mark 6 or 200 c for 25 minutes.

Now to serve

- Serve with fresh vegetables or my favorite baked beans.

CHICKEN, LEEK AND HAM PIE
(serves 4)

Shopping list

- 3x chicken breasts (use quorn and vegetable stock for vegetarian version)
- 4oz good ham
- 1 leek
- 1 clove of garlic
- 1pk puff pastry
- 3oz flour
- 1 chicken stock cube
- 1 small pot double cream
- 1 egg
- 2oz butter
- Salt and pepper
- 1 tub of dried sage

Family Meals

Now to prepare:

- Cut up the chicken into 1" dice
- Chop up the ham into medium sized slices
- Chop the leek into ½" rings and wash and drain
- Peel and chop garlic
- Dissolve the stock cube into 1pt of boiling water
- Crack an egg and whisk with a fork

Now let's get cooking!

- In a large saucepan heat the butter over a medium heat, then add chopped chicken and fry for 5 minutes; then add the leeks, ham and garlic.
- Continue cooking for 3 minutes, stirring occasionally.
- Add the flour to the pan and stir in thoroughly.
- Add the stock and stir until mixture thickens, then add 1 teaspoon of sage.
- Simmer for 10 minutes over a low heat, add salt and pepper to taste, then pour mixture into ovenproof dish (approx 10"x8").

- Roll out pastry on a lightly floured surface, making the pastry just slightly bigger than the dish.
- Cover pie with the pastry; then brush with the beaten egg.
- Bake in oven on gas mark6 or 200 c for approx 15-20 minutes until pastry is risen and golden.

Now to serve:

- Serve with chips, mash or new potatoes and peas.

Family Meals

SIMPLE CHEAT'S MINTY LAMB CASSEROLE

Shopping list

- 400g lean diced lamb
- 4 carrots
- 1 leek
- 2 celery sticks
- 1 lamb stock cube
- 1oz gravy granules
- 2 dessert spoons of mint sauce

To prepare:

- Preheat oven on gas mark 3 or 170c
- Peel and dice the carrots (1cm size pieces)
- Cut the leek into 1" rings and wash and drain
- Slice the celery sticks into 1cm pieces
- Dissolve stock cube in 1pt of boiling water

Now get cooking!

- Put the lamb and vegetables into a casserole dish and mix together.

- Using the stock, add the gravy granules and stir until it forms a gravy; add in the mint sauce.

- Pour the gravy mixture over the lamb and vegetables in the casserole dish, cover the casserole and cook in oven for 1 ½ hours. Then remove and stir and cook for a further 20 minutes.

Now to serve:

- Serve with mashed potatoes.

Desserts

WICKED, naughty but nice, a real treat—yes, desserts are very special.

Desserts are something we all like to treat ourselves to. We can be healthy and go for the fruit salad or be just plain naughty and have that double chocolate gateaux with chocolate sauce and double cream.

Desserts can be easily bought in any supermarket laden with calories, easy to serve. You can buy them fresh from the chiller counter or cake counter at the supermarket, or frozen in the freezer aisles—the choice is unbelievable. They are full of calories, E-numbers and are waiting to be eaten.

Farm shops sell homemade cakes and pies, which are also very good as a treat.

But if you fancy your hand at a few simple desserts that you can make at home and that won't break the bank and are just a good to eat, try Tim's desserts as a homemade alternative.

Here are some of Tim's delicious recipes for dessert:

GRILLED CHOCOLATE PEACHES
(serves 4)

Shopping list

- 2 x ripe peaches
- 50g plain chocolate
- 1 small pot of Greek yoghurt
- 4 teaspoons demerara sugar

Now to get prepared:

- Slice the peaches in and remove stones
- Grate chocolate

Now to get cooking!

- Pre-heat the grill on a high heat.
- Place the peach ½'s on a tray, cut side up.
- Divide the grated chocolate between the 1/2s, placing in the hollow.
- Add a dessert spoon of yoghurt, and a teaspoon of sugar to each peach half, and grill for 4-5 minutes until sugar has dissolved and is bubbling, then serve.

Now to serve:

- Serve with ice cream.

BAKED LEMON PUDDING
(serves 4-6)

Shopping list

- 1 ½ oz butter
- 3 oz soft brown sugar
- 1 lemon
- 2 eggs
- 3oz self raising flour
- 250ml semi skimmed milk

Now to get prepared:

- Pre heat oven to gas mark 6 or 200 c
- Zest the lemon (grated lemon peel), then juice the lemon (squeeze)
- Separate the eggs keeping both the yolks and the whites (clear liquid) separate.

Now to get cooking!

- In a mixing bowl cream together the butter, sugar and lemon zest until a white colour.
- Beat the egg yolks in a small bowl. Then add to the mixture stir through gently, then fold in flour and stir well.
- Add the milk and juice and stir until it forms a smooth batter.
- Whisk the egg whites in a separate bowl until peaked; fold into mixture.
- Place the mixture into a ceramic dish (approx 8"x6"), then place this into a roasting tin with about 1 ½" of water in the bottom.
- Cook in oven for 30 minutes until sponge is firm and springy.

Now to serve:

- Scoop out portions and serve with custard or cream.

RHUBARB FOOL
(serves 2)

Shopping list

- 225g fresh rhubarb
- 40g demerara sugar
- 1 orange
- 100 ml double cream
- 1 tablespoon of water

Now to get prepared:

- Cut rhubarb into 1" pieces
- Zest the orange

Now to get cooking!

- Place the rhubarb, orange zest (grated orange peel) and water in a small saucepan and simmer over a low heat for 15 minutes until rhubarb is soft, drain and set aside to cool.

- Whip up the cream until thick and fold into cold rhubarb.

- Divide mixture between 2 wine glasses and chill for 1 hour.

Now to serve:

- Serve with shortbread or almond biscuits.

Desserts

APPLE AND RASPBERRY CRUMBLE
(serves 4-6)

Shopping list

- 3 oz plain flour
- 2 oz butter (soft)
- 6 tablespoons of demerara sugar
- 1 oz ground almonds
- 6 oz fresh or frozen raspberries
- 1lb 2 oz cooking apples

Now to get prepared:

- Peel and cut the apples into chunks (1")
- Pre heat oven to gas mark 5 or 190 c
- Tip the flour into a mixing bowl, add soft butter and using your fingertips, rub it in until it looks like breadcrumbs.
- Stir in almonds and add 2 tablespoons of the sugar, mix, then set aside.

Now to get cooking!

- In a saucepan put in apples, 2 tablespoons of the sugar and 2 spoons of water.

- Cook on a medium heat for 5 minutes, then stir in raspberries.
- Place the mixture into an oven proof dish; then add crumble topping evenly.
- Bake in the oven for 20 minutes until crumble is golden.

Now to serve:

- Serve hot or cold with custard, cream or ice cream.

Desserts

COCONUT RICE PUDDING
(serves 4)

Shopping list

- 900ml Milk
- 3 tablespoons of coconut milk
- 1 teaspoon of mixed spice
- 75g pudding rice
- 25g of demerara sugar

Now to get cooking!

- Place the milk, and coconut milk and spices in a saucepan and heat.
- Stir in the rice and sugar and bring to the boil. Leave to simmer for 30 minutes, stirring occasionally until the rice has thickened and cooked.

Now to serve:

- Serve hot or cold
- Add a swirl of raspberry puree

BREAD AND BUTTER PUDDING

Shopping list

- 8 slices of white bread
- 50g butter
- 50g dried fruit
- 40g caster sugar
- 2 large eggs
- 450ml of milk
- 150ml whipping cream

To prepare:

- Pre heat oven to 170oc / gas mark 3.
- Remove the crusts from the bread and spread with butter and cut into small triangles.
- Place half the bread in the base of the dish and sprinkle dried fruit and half the caster sugar.
- Top with the remaining bread buttered side up and sprinkle the remaining sugar on top.

- Whisk the eggs with the milk and cream and pour over the pudding.

- Leave for 30minutes to allow the bread to absorb the liquid.

Now get cooking!

- Place in a roasting tin and pour in enough boiling water to come half way up the sides of the dish.

- Bake in the preheated oven for 50-60 minutes until the pudding is set and the top is golden.

Now to serve:

- Accompany with custard, ice cream or fresh cream.

A Special Meal for Two!

Posh nosh—a romantic meal for two!

♣

STARTER

Grilled Portobello mushroom with melted goats cheese and tomato chutney

Shopping list

- 2 large flat Portobello mushrooms
- 1 x 3oz piece of goat's cheese
- 1 jar of good tomato chutney
- 1 bag of rocket leaves
- Salt and pepper
- Olive oil

To prepare:

- Grate the cheese
- Wash off rocket leaves, shake off excess water
- Pre-heat grill on high heat

Now get cooking!

- Place mushrooms onto a baking tray, sprinkle with salt and pepper; then drizzle with olive oil; then add a spoonful of tomato chutney.
- Grill for 4 minutes, remove the tray and divide cheese between the mushrooms and return to grill for 2 minutes.
- Place mushrooms on plates; serve with some rocket salad and finally drizzle with olive oil.

♣

MAIN COURSE

Baked supreme of chicken, spring onion mash, wilted spinach and tarragon and white wine cream.

A Special Meal for Two

Shopping list

- 2x skinless chicken breasts
- 1 bunch of spring onions
- 1 bag of washed spinach
- 2 large potatoes
- 1 tub dried tarragon
- 200mls of double cream
- 1 glass medium white wine
- 2 oz butter
- Salt and pepper
- Olive oil
- 2oz butter

To prepare:

- Peel and dice the potatoes
- Cut off ends of spring onions and chop into 1/2cm pieces
- Pre-heat oven to gas mark7 or 220 c

Now to get cooking!

- In a large saucepan place potatoes and cover with boiling salted hot water and then boil until potatoes are soft.

- In the meantime in a frying pan heat 1 dessert spoon of oil and place in the chicken pieces; then cook for 2 minutes on both sides until starting to colour.

- Place the chicken in oven and cook for a further 10-12 minutes depending on chicken breast size.

- Once chicken is cooked, remove from pan and keep warm.

- In the pan you cooked the chicken, add white wine and simmer until it has reduced by half; then add ½ teaspoon of tarragon and the cream; add a sprinkle of salt and simmer for approx 3 minutes until thickened. Check seasoning and adjust if necessary.

- In a medium size saucepan melt ½ the butter, add the spinach and cook until wilted; add a sprinkle of salt and pepper and cover with a lid.

- Drain the potatoes; then mash with the rest of the butter. Add spring onions; check seasoning—adjust if required.

A Special Meal for Two

Now to serve:

- Place a mound of potato in centre of plates; slice the chicken and fan on top of potato; divide the spinach in ½ and squeeze excess juice out before placing by potatoes; then cover chicken with sauce.

- Accompany with extra vegetables if required.

♣

PUDDING

Poached spiced pears

Shopping list

- 1 large pear
- 1 lemon
- 1 jar stem ginger
- 1 tub cardamom pods
- 1 teaspoon of sugar

Now to get prepared

- Peel the pear; then ½ it, take out core.
- Juice the lemon, and then toss the pears in it to prevent browning.
- Slice 1 nugget of ginger finely.

Now to get cooking!

- In a small saucepan place the pear into ½ pt of water; add 3 cardamom pods, the sugar, the ginger and 4 dessert spoons of syrup from the ginger jar; then poach for 12-15 minutes until tender.

- Transfer the pears using a holey spoon; boil remaining liquid for 4-5 minutes until it becomes syrupy; place pears back in and leave to cool.

Now to serve

- Place on plates, drizzle with juice and serve.

- Accompany with whipped cream, ice cream or Greek yoghurt.

Kids' Lunch Boxes

THIS is really important—get this wrong and you are really in trouble!

Kids' lunch boxes carry 'street cred'—that means the children at school always look at what is in each other's lunch box. They even swop things, so you had better get it right.

Kids will swop what you have packed, pick at it, throw it in the bin and pretend they have eaten it; or if you are really lucky, eat it.

Lunch boxes can work out very expensive if you are not really sure what your child really eats, and not what you think they should eat. That is not to say you should not try new things, but be realistic—otherwise you are just throwing your money in the school bin.

Carbohydrates are an important energy source, and kids need lots of energy. Sandwiches in the lunch box are a basic item. But you can also be inventive by using small rolls of different types of breads, brown seeded whole meal (you can buy bags containing mixed rolls, which is good for them to try); also, you could experiment with filling pitta bread or wraps.

Use a wide variety of filling over the week and always put at least two choices in their boxes; that way they may eat one or swop one. Either way at least they are having something at lunch time

Ideas for fillings:

- Chopped banana
- Cheese and tomato
- Jam
- Peanut butter
- Chicken with salad
- Tuna and sweet corn
- Spicy mixed veg wrap
- Egg (but not if they have had egg for breakfast)

Remember, this is their lunch box, not yours—so remember what they really like to eat and don't make this 'the battle of the lunch box'. Add new things as well as putting in things you know they like.

Those little extras

Healthy snacks

- A portion of fresh fruit. Bananas, Apples, Grapes, Satsumas, are easy to carry and eat. But remember, whatever the fruit, it's got to get to school in that lunch box that might be thrown across the playground before it gets to lunchtime.

- A packet of raisins: most kids love them and they come in multipacks.

- Yogurts or small pots of rice pudding.

- Nibbles, carrot sticks, fish sticks, cheese sticks, celery—yes, you get the idea: anything they can munch on or easily swop with their friends is great.

- Crisps. Well, all kids love them. Just read the labels and watch out for e-numbers with added salt. If you can try the mixed vegetable ones, that way they are trying things like beetroot and parsnip without them even knowing.

- Make sure your child drinks plenty of fluid so he or she is well hydrated. Try to avoid fizzy drinks. These often contain e-numbers: loads of sugar, and will make the kids go wild. Apart from that, they are bad for teeth. Instead, pack a bottle of still or sparkling water, unsweetened fruit juice or milk. Make sure the bottles are non-breakable.

When they come home from school don't be surprised if they haven't eaten everything or even anything; remember, they have the important job of playing, are learning new skills, so eating is low on their list of priorities. Praise them foe what they have eaten, and remember what has been eaten, for future reference.

Try and remember, children don't eat as much as grown ups, so think small portions!

When shopping for the lunch boxes don't forget to buy containers or food bags and plastic spoons.

Tips

WHEN you are cooking for someone else you should try and be aware of any health issues that can affect what he or she can eat.

Things you may have to take into consideration could be:

- Diabetic
- Cholesterol
- Wheat allergies
- Allergies to dairy products
- Nut allergies.

Information on healthy eating and special diets is available at www.nhsdirect.nhs.uk

Easy prepared vegetables

Fresh Vegetables really are good for you, and if you find all that peeling and chopping a bit much, you can find the hard bit already done for you, if you look at the supermarkets. They have trays of freshly chopped and peeled vegetables. With the bonus that there is no waste, you can see exactly how big portions there are in each pack and they are ready to boil or stir-fry.

Extras for those desserts

Just to finish off those special desserts, you might like to add custard. This can come in various forms, the sort you mix and then boil with milk in a pan. Be warned—it can go lumpy, very thick or very thin if you get it wrong. Or there is the easy way. Try packets. Just mix with boiling water, ready made in a carton which you just heat and pour. If you fancy, there is fresh cream, pouring, whipping extra thick all in cartons from the chiller counter; or squirty cream in a can (kids love that). Or Fromage Frais, with less calories.

Bargain buys at the supermarkets

Whoopsed (items marked with a yellow label) can become your favourite word; it's a way of getting something special at bargain price, and maybe trying out something new. It's a great way to shop as long as you put whatever you have bought on tonight's menu. 'B.O.G.O. F.' —buy one, get one free: but just think, do you really need it? Are you going to use it? Or are you just spending too much of the household budget on something you don't really need?

Roll a lemon/orange in your hands before using; it makes it easier to squeeze when cut.

Overripe bananas: mash them with a fork, then serve on toast and sprinkle with cinnamon for a healthy breakfast.

Bananas should always be stored away from other fruits and will actually keep firmer for longer if they are left in the plastic bag.

To stop a banana going brown once peeled, just place the banana while still in its skin in a jug of boiling water for 15 seconds; then peel and use as normal for sandwiches and fruit salads.

Limp lettuce can be revived by placing the lettuce leaves in a bowl of cold water with a peeled sliced potato; leave to soak for a short while, then rinse, dry and use as normal.

To stop lettuce leaves going brown, use a plastic knife to cut the leaves.

Fromage Frais you can use to:

- Thicken soups and sauces such as curry sauce.
- Instead of butter in mashed potatoes.
- Instead of cream on desserts; you can add sweetener to it if you prefer.

Carrots keep better if you cut off the top and bottoms, then place in an airtight container in the fridge.

Bread:

- When buying French sticks, buy a long one—it's cheaper. Then cut into portions and freeze the ones you don't want to keep for next time. When you do need one, just pop in the oven to re-heat.
- To keep your bread fresh, store in a plastic bag. Make sure you twist the bag and remove all the air before sealing.
- Sandwich crusts and the last slice of the bread should be stored in a plastic container, then turned into bread crumbs.

Understanding labels

'Use by'

'Use by': **NEVER EAT** products after this date, and follow the storage instructions. However, check to see if the food can be frozen if you need to eat it at a later date.

'Best before'

'Best before': these dates refer to quality rather than food safety. Foods with a 'best before' date should be safe to eat after the 'best before' date, but they may no longer be at their best. One exception is eggs. **NEVER EAT EGGS after the 'Best before' date.**

About our Chef

Tim Johns

WELL, our chef is the real expert—he has been a chef for twenty years. He has worked in large hotels and restaurants, catering for a wide variety of customers, from special occasions such as weddings, corporate functions as well as preparing superb food for special meals.

He designs his menus with flare and uses his extensive knowledge and creative skills to make his meals nutritious and inventive. His menus have been featured in *Taste of the Shires* (Kaffe Frederique's recipe section).

He has designed these recipes especially for the beginner who would like to try his/her hand at real cooking. Each menu contains a shopping list and an easy-to-follow menu. They are simple recipes providing healthy nutritious meals, which are easy to prepare, and delicious to eat.

Consideration has been given to the culinary language, the type of cooking implements that are required and the cooking times.

His aim was to introduce a novice cook to the world of cooking, making it an easy and enjoyable experience for a man who was suddenly thrown into the role of chef for himself and his family.

Enjoy cooking!